SELAH

*300 Inspirational Proverbs, Quotes, Reflections
and Meditations to Motivate and Empower
You to Think with a Kingdom Mind-set*

JERMAINE VAUGHN

WESTBOW
PRESS®
A DIVISION OF THOMAS NELSON
& ZONDERVAN

WestBow Press books may be ordered through booksellers or by contacting:

WestBow Press
A Division of Thomas Nelson & Zondervan
1663 Liberty Drive
Bloomington, IN 47403
www.westbowpress.com
1 (866) 928-1240

Scripture quotations taken from the Amplified® Bible (AMP), Copyright © 2015 by The Lockman Foundation Used by permission. www.Lockman.org

Scripture taken from the New King James Version®. Copyright © 1982 by Thomas Nelson. Used by permission. All rights reserved.

Scripture quotations are from The ESV® Bible (The Holy Bible, English Standard Version®), copyright © 2001 by Crossway, a publishing ministry of Good News Publishers. Used by permission. All rights reserved.

ISBN: 978-1-9736-1425-8 (sc)
ISBN: 978-1-9736-1427-2 (hc)
ISBN: 978-1-9736-1426-5 (e)

Library of Congress Control Number: 2018900321

Print information available on the last page.

WestBow Press rev. date: 1/26/2018

CONTENTS

Acknowledgements

First, I'd like to acknowledge and thank God for bringing me to this point today. God's grace, mercy, and favor have truly worked in harmony throughout my life, and I thank Him for keeping me throughout the years. I thank Him for not only saving me but revealing my destiny and purpose.

I'd also like to thank my parents, Jimmy and Bridget Vaughn, who encouraged me from a very early age to think critically for myself.

I want to also thank my wife, Evelyn Vaughn, who encourages and inspires me daily to pursue my dreams and purpose. She has also given me legacy through our precious children whom we love with all our hearts. I dedicate my first published book to these people whom I love dearly.

Last, I would like to thank the people who will read this book. Your support and interest in what I have to say means more than you know. Thank you!

INTRODUCTION

The meaning of the word "Selah" itself is a mystery. The exact interpretation and etymology of the word are debated. However, there is enough consistency among interpretations to conclude a general meaning. "Selah" is a word that suggests validity, importance, and truth. "Selah" is also a musical term that denotes a musical interlude, pause, or break *before moving on* to the next verse. The Amplified Bible interprets Selah as "pause, and think of that." It is also understood as "stop, listen, and think." Another interpretation can be to "stop, to measure and weigh something."

Throughout the years, Jermaine has developed a reputation for wisdom that provokes thought and challenges paradigms that keep people from living a progressive life. This book is a collection of proverbial writing meant to inspire you, yet challenge you to think at a higher level—with a Kingdom mindset.

In this book you'll find a compilation of 300 of the most inspirational proverbs, quotes, reflections, and meditations from Jermaine's journal. This collection covers nearly 10 years of notes.

You can read one entry daily as a devotional or all entries at the same time. I pray that as you read you'll be provoked to stop, think, and reevaluate.

I pray you are blessed!
God Bless.

PART I
SELAH
QUOTES AND PROVERBS

Romans 12:2 New King James Version
And do not be conformed to this world, but be transformed
by the *renewing of your* **mind**, that you may prove what
is that good and acceptable and perfect will of God

01 Time is one of the more valuable things in life. You have none to spare, and you have none to waste. It must be spent with intention and purpose.

02 According to research people's greatest regrets in life aren't the things they've done but wish they hadn't. People's greatest regrets in life are those things people wish they did but never found the courage to do until it was too late.

03 If all your goals can be accomplished in your lifetime alone, then you have lived a selfish life and your vision is too small and short sighted. Will younger generations catch on to your vision and carry it to another level, or will it die when you do?

04 Jesus didn't come to die. He came to defeat death. He never intended to stay in the grave. His intention was to tame death and the grave.

05 When you succeed at copying someone else's assignment, you fail at completing your own.

06 What people recommend you for is evidence of your gift.

07 Jesus not only died for you. He died as you. Therefore, not only do you live for Him, you live as Him on the earth. He died as a representative of you. You live as a representative of Him.

08 If you follow Christ, He will in turn lead you to people. That's His nature.

09 Your purpose is God given. That means it is tailor-made by God Himself to suit you.

10 What you *do* or *don't do* now will have an impact generations to come.

11 If you aim low, then don't have high expectations.

12 Some of us pray for clarity when in fact it's not clarity that we need—it's trust!

13 Is it really that we don't have enough, or do we simply misuse what we have?

14 Most of the time it's not that we've failed it's really that we've quit too soon. Difficulty, obstacles and challenges are not an indication of failure.

15 Let the things that you don't want to become motivate you for the better.

16 God is not looking for you to get it 100-percent right; He is looking for you to commit 100 percent so that He can bless you 100 fold.

17 Division is the enemy to "the vision." Die-vision.

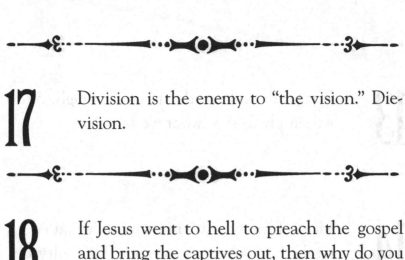

18 If Jesus went to hell to preach the gospel and bring the captives out, then why do you complain about your assignment? Are you greater than He is?

19 The question is not "Am I ready?" The question that truly matters is "Am I willing?" Am I committed?

20 Don't just hold high standards for yourself. Also hold high standards for those you call friends.

21 Sometimes in order to go higher in life you must get rid of some "nouns"—people, places, and things!

22 Put your best foot forward or don't put one forward at all. No half stepping allowed.

23 Playing it safe often kills the momentum of progress. Every now and then you have to call a blitz and go for it!

24 Those who are *sitting* doing nothing oftentimes tell you not to *stand* for anything.

25 Where you're going is much more significant than where you came from. There are no limits for you!

26 It would be a shame for God to call you— and for you to miss the call. Focus!

27 Comfortability and Conformity should be synonymous. The moment we refuse to leave our comfort zone to achieve our purpose and pursue our dream we have just chosen to become like everyone else.

28 You will never make a decision that affects you only. Believe it or not, every decision you make or fail to make affects someone else! The choices you make are beneficial or detrimental to another in the present time or in the future!

29 You can't use the time you have lost. You can't use the time you have wasted. The only thing you can use is the time you have left! What are you going to do with the time you have left?

30 Preparing to win isn't fun, but the reward of winning because you've prepared is. Champions put in the work.

31 God has not changed his mind about you. Period!

32 Jesus did not come to bring the religion of Christianity. He came to bring the kingdom of God to the earth, a royal nation of kings and priests to rule His earth well. (1 Peter 2:9).

33 When you *give* you are changing somebody's current situation. When you *empower* you are changing somebody's life.

34 Every success story involves some type of risk. Yes, if you go for it you may fail, but if you *never* go for it you have failed already.

35 The soul of another person is depending on you getting in your God-ordained position. If you don't complete your assignment, not only will you fail the assignment but you will fail the people attached to it.

36 Don't allow the blows of life to knock the potential and passion out of you.

37 Don't let people who never try anything talk you out of trying something. Go for it— dreams become reality when you take some real risk!

38 Don't just view risk as a possibility of failing. Also view it as a possibility of succeeding! Change your focus from "what if it doesn't work" to "what if this works".

39 Wishing in and of itself is a waste of time. Your wishes must graduate into your will.

40 Grace is not only the privilege to be forgiven; it is also the empowerment to remain faithful.

41 Being in unity does not mean you abandon your uniqueness. It is diversity on one accord that creates the harmony to *make a difference.*

42 If a husband doesn't align himself under God, then how can he demand that his wife effectively align herself under his leadership?

43 Will you continue to wait for opportunity to introduce itself or will you find the heart to introduce yourself to opportunity?

44 When you begin to doubt, you have to revisit your testimony and realize that God has always been faithful.

45 I love history. However, I love the future much more. Sometime we have to part ways with our past so that we can stay faithful to our future. Look forward!

46 The will of democracy begins with "We the People." The will of God's kingdom begins with "Thus Saith the Lord!" It requires obedience to accomplish.

47 It can only get darker when light is taken away. Don't dim down shine brighter.

48 Dwell in unity but stay unique. God made you this way.

49 If you have big dreams, you must have big plans to accompany them.

50 Man can never demote who or what God chooses to promote.

51 Yes, you see the problem. The question is, do you see yourself as part of the solution?

52 All the darkness in the world can't hide the light of a single candle. Light is *always* more powerful than darkness.

53 What you've been asking for and praying for—can God trust you with it?

54 True leaders possess the ability to pull the potential out of others. In other words, *they bring out the best in everybody.*

55 He who never takes risk will never reach his full potential. Every success story was first an opportunity before it ever became a possibility.

56 Just as a flower buds and then blossoms into its glory, so should your *character* while you are pursuing purpose!

57 It is not my ability that earns grace, it is His grace that gives me ability.

58 The father of success is work. The mother of achievement is ambition. Keep working hard and keep believing until the concept is birthed.

59 A true friend will tell you the truth—not to prevent your life, but to progress your life.

60 Success is measured by reaching *your* maximum potential not the maximum potential people think you have. Be careful not to allow the limitations of others limit you.

61 So many of us live our whole lives on the defensive; try being on the offensive, and try to be proactive rather than reactive. Take a risk and live life to your fullest potential.

62 The cross is the key to the kingdom; without the cross, there is *no access* to the kingdom!

63 There is no such thing as a barren believer. We produce fruit.

64 Jesus saved you not only so that you can be with Him one day; He saved you so that you may have the power to take him to others (John 17:15–18).

65 Why compete with one another when you could complement (complete) one another?

66 Opportunity will rarely come to you. While positioning yourself you'll meet opportunity, and when you meet it, it's up to you to seize it.

67 Success can't be an option; it must be the conclusion.

68 If you're not careful, you can be in bondage to your comfort zone. You can actually be paralyzed and captive to the idea of being safe.

69 You cannot influence whom you avoid.

70 Just because you've taken some blows or even lost one round doesn't mean you've lost the fight. You've got more rounds to go. Keep going.

71 What time does church start? Answer: once we leave the building.

72 The only people who will have a problem with you pursuing and living in the reality of your dreams are those who are living in the nightmare of never pursuing theirs.

73 Don't allow anyone to have *control* over your life who has shown no *commitment* in your life. No investment means no equity.

74 *Sound* captures people and piques their interests. *Noise*, on the other hand, irritates people and turns them away. When you open your mouth, which one are you making with the *voice* God has given you?

75 So asking people to come to your church hasn't been successful, huh? Try asking your church to go to the people.

76 You have the Holy Spirit not only to release a praise from heaven—or even to discern right and wrong. You have the Holy Spirit so that you may be an effective *witness* (John 15:26–27).

77 Rebuke is ultimately for restoration not retaliation—so that there's repentance, not so that there's revenge. God's will is reconciliation.

78 In order to have an impact on communities, we (the church) must first become a community.

79 Works are the fruit of your salvation, not the prerequisite to your salvation."

80 Don't listen to the phrase, "It's never been done before." Be the first to do it.

81 If you're not careful you could easily mistake a pigeon for a dove.

82 When you make it your business to build a community, a community will make it its business to build you. Don't forget to care for people.

83 The number one person that needs to be convinced of who you are is you.

84 Waiting doesn't mean to sit there and do nothing.

85 God made crickets to respond to critics so you wouldn't have to. You stay focused!

86 The sign of good leaders is not that they are in power; it's the fruition of those they've empowered. Leaders leave legacies.

87 Your gifts are to be given to the next generation. Pass them on.

88 Pursue your dreams to such a degree that retreat is not an option. Literally commit to the point of no return!

89 Time is too valuable to waste on trivial matters.

90 Gold doesn't get glory until it has been through the fire.

91 Most will come around when they want or need something from you. But there's a few that come around strictly because *you* are what they want and need most. Don't forget to appreciate the few in your life.

92 If you are unwilling to sacrifice then you are unwilling to succeed.

93 Your gift has a purpose attached to it.

94 The mandate is to go and send.

95 Man, if you don't even know who you are then what business do you have giving a woman your name?

96 People will say it's never been done. Smile and tell them to stay tuned.

97 If you are under the New Covenant, you have an advocate with a Father, not a judge.

98 Good is unacceptable when great is attainable.

99 It doesn't worry me when I'm faced with problems. The problem should be worried that it's faced with a solution.

100 There are those who sit on opportunity, and there are those who seize opportunity."

101 You must move your dreams from concept to conception. Give life to your ideas. Take action!

102 You are not being punished, you are being prepared. It's a process.

103 The enemy of truth is not lies, it's silence.

104 Kingdom people never focus on getting into heaven. They are too focused on manifesting the fact that heaven got into them.

105 We often want someone's level of success absent their level of sacrifice.

106 The Kingdom doesn't seek members. Citizens and sons are its fruit.

107 Nearly every move of God in scripture was not in a church building.

108 Rest assured that nothing or no one can revoke the promises and destiny God spoke concerning you.

Isaiah 55:11 New International Version
so is my word that goes out from my mouth: It will not return to me empty, but will accomplish what I desire and achieve the purpose for which I sent it.

109 In order for you to see the rainbow, you must have been present during the storm.

110 Hell was not originally made for us. Eden was crafted for us.

111 If you're going through Hell, just make sure to come out of it on fire!

112 Missions is not drive through, wave goodbye, see you later. It's more like dig in, anchor down, plow, and plant.

113 The possibility of failure is no valid reason to never try. Remember, it's also possible that you will succeed.

114 When you take a risk, you free yourself from the mental prison of *what if.*

115 God does not reveal your imperfections to drive you away from Him, but rather to draw you nearer to Him.

116 The underdog has nothing to lose and everything to gain. Change your perspective. Go for it!

117 How could someone truly love you if you constantly pretend to be someone you're not?

118 Just because you have something in common doesn't necessarily mean you have chemistry.

119 Antichange and antigrowth should be synonyms. If nothing changes then nothing grows.

120 Liberty without order or boundaries is simply anarchy.

121 Living a life without discipline leads to destruction. Living a life full of discipline leads to destiny.

122 Don't seek position. Instead seek God's purpose, and that purpose will ultimately place you in a position that can never be revoked by man.

123 You should absolutely expect to succeed. Failing is not an option for you. You may struggle, but in the end you *will* win!

124 You rarely attain victory while simultaneously thinking like a victim.

125 God forgave you, why can't you forgive yourself?

126 If God forgave them, then why can't you?

127 There is no time to live aimlessly. Live purposely and precisely.

128 The only cure to your passion is fulfillment! You won't have true peace until you answer that special thing that's been calling you. It's calling you to *become*.

129 You are the gift God wants to give into someone's life!

130 You don't have to do everything perfectly, but everything must be done excellently.

131 Don't just count the cost also count the benefit. Don't just ask yourself "is it worth the sacrifice?" Also ask yourself "what is the sacrifice worth?"

132 The small things you do make a big difference to somebody. You are relevant!

133 Many wear the cross around their necks, but few are willing to carry one on their back!

134 God created you to be the solution. Ephesians 3:20

135 Your action activates your faith. James 2:14-26

136 People will either love you for the truth or hate you for it. However, that's not your decision to make.

137 Jesus' purpose for coming into the world was to pardon you, not to punish you. John 3:16-17

138 Move from having the potential to having the capacity. Develop what's already inside of you.

139 Death isn't the worst thing that can happen to you. The worst thing that can happen to you is allowing yourself to die inside while you're still alive.

140 In order to succeed you have to take the risk of failing.

141 The Gospel of Christ spiritually raises dead souls.

142 The *decision* to accomplish something is more powerful than the logic of how you're going to accomplish it.

143 It's not how good we are, it's how good he is.

144 Never take advice from those who always point out problems but never propose solutions.

145 Oftentimes the ones who sabotage your success are those you've let into your inner circle.

146 Whatever takes work to achieve also takes work to maintain.

147 Never allow others to make you feel guilty about a passion that was given by God.

148 Don't complain about how dark it is. Darkness is simply the absence of light. Maybe you just need to show up and shine! Matthew 5:13-16

149 The Church has been given the ministry of reconciliation not of retaliation.

150 Ironically enough, although dreams are directly related to sleep you can never share them with those who are in a state of slumber.

151 You think they left you but God actually freed you from them.

152 We are the only creation God made in His own image and likeness.

153 Dreams happen in the comfort of your bed, but they definitely can't come true there.

154 You can't change anything from the outside looking in. You must involve yourself.

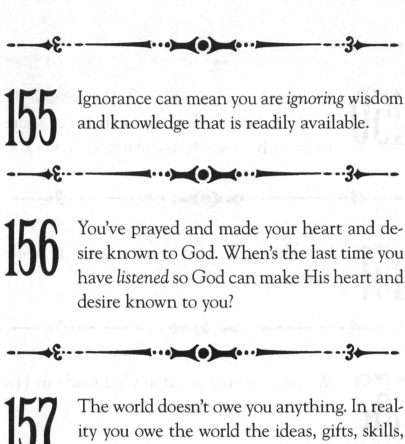

155 Ignorance can mean you are *ignoring* wisdom and knowledge that is readily available.

156 You've prayed and made your heart and desire known to God. When's the last time you have *listened* so God can make His heart and desire known to you?

157 The world doesn't owe you anything. In reality you owe the world the ideas, gifts, skills, and talents God placed inside of you. Make your deposit.

158 Nevertheless, the lesser is never an option.

159 Sometimes truth comforts you, other times truth confronts you. Either way it's all good for you.

160 David didn't cease being king just because he fell. Don't let circumstances make you forget who you really are.

161 Sometimes it's not that something has *power* over us as much as it has *permission* from us. Be intentional about what you allow!

162 Outstanding means to stand out, distinct from the norm.

163 Knowledge reveals the power that is already within you. Discover who you truly are, or you'll believe any and every fairy tale spoken concerning you.

164 Great leadership empowers you and deploys you.

165 Great leaders *enable*. Poor leaders *disable*.

166 What good is success if you don't give back and lift others up?

167 Everything that stops or slows growth in your life falls under one of the following categories.

- Fear
- Complacency
- Laziness
- Neglect
- Procrastination
- Rebellion

168 Don't focus so much on the fact that you are the least common denominator that you forget that you are part of the equation. You are a variable in God's formula.

169 The Lord wins the battle and gives us the victory. 2 Chronicles 20:15

170 You may experience some danger and darkness outside the will of God, but in the will of God you are dangerous in the midst of darkness."

171 Light travels faster than sound; however, both your life and voice should echo to enlighten and empower others.

172 The life of the believer is similar to the game of chess. Make it your business to pursue the King!

173 Where there is no truth, there is no change. In order to grow, we must embrace both the *amen* and the *ouch!*

174 Success is like a comma, not a period. It is not a stopping point. Keep going!

175 I've been told that in order for a marriage to work, both people will have to give 50/50. But I've learned that in order for one to last it takes 100/100. Give your all.

176 Are you an asset or a liability to your team?

177 You don't have to earn grace, it is granted. You don't have to deserve mercy, it is the giver's desire.

178 A fan's loyalty to you is contingent on your good performance. A friend's loyalty is based on the essence of who you are as a person. Are you a fan of God or a friend of God?

179 Those on your team must be just as passionate and just as convinced as you are about the goal and the vision.

180 Ambition is the courage to get started on your dreams. Determination is the commitment to finish once you have started.

181 There is the right way and there is the easy way. One pays off in the end; the other you'll have to pay for in the end.

182 Being relevant does not mean you must compromise, and staying true does not mean you must become out of touch.

183 Lust feels like love until it's time to make a sacrifice or commit.

184 Many of us desire to be instruments used of God, but we don't want to allow God to fine-tune us. As a result, many of us are out there just making noise.

185 Brave means to act in spite of the presence or feeling of fear.

186 Without the resurrection of Christ, you would be accountable for all your sin. Thank God for Jesus!

187 God makes beauty out of a harsh past.

188 It's time for a response to the God given ability he placed inside of you. Today is the day to *respond* because you are well *able*. Take Responsibility today!

189 Ability means to be ready and able. To have the ability means you can accomplish the task and perform at a maximum level at any time.

190 Capability is possessing the potential capacity to operate or do something. To be capable means that you naturally have the gift, but your skill or talent can be developed to a higher level. Literally, you have additional room to be filled to the max.

191 Potential is the capacity to be potent. Literally, a reservoir of purpose and power.

192 Opposition is that which opposes your rightful position. Or living in a manner which is opposite to the position God created for you.

193 When God places you into position, there will be those that tell you that you don't belong where you are. Don't let it bother you, they weren't sent by Him.

194 Opportunity will oftentimes be accompanied with opposition. Focus!

195 Laziness may be convenient in the beginning, but it ends up causing more work in the long run. A shortcut today is a headache tomorrow.

196 The favor of God can take you places that your merit cannot. When God's favor is on you, there is nothing anyone can do to revoke it.

197 We often find every excuse not to do something. In order for change to occur, we have to find every excuse to do the things we don't want to do, but know we need to do.

198 It's great to learn from others but it's dangerous to compare yourself to others.

199 People who succeed interpret mistakes and failures as learning lessons. People who will not succeed are those who interpret mistakes and failures as a sign or permission to quit.

200 When you hide your identity so deeply in the thoughts, ideas, and approval of others, you subsequently bury the very thing God wants to reveal to the world through you. Become the best you.

201 If you can't name at least one thing you specialize in or do with excellence, then chances are you are doing too much and need to focus on something specific.

202 There are some things you can accomplish with talent, but there are other things that you will never accomplish without the anointing.

203 You can't quit during the investment period.

204 It doesn't matter whether you barely make it. The fact that remains is you made it.

205 Some will see disaster, others will see opportunity. Which are you?

206 The first step to making change is buying into the idea of owning the responsibility to change.

207 What good is knowledge if it's never applied?

208 Where there is no action there should be no expectation.

209 *Conviction* and *convinced* are derived from the same etymology. To have a conviction means your subconscious soul is convinced of a purpose God placed inside of you. There's a reason it pulls at you. Don't ignore it.

210 People will say, "You need to slow down." Your reply should be, "Maybe you need to catch up."

211 You will never convince sheep to hunt. They will never leave the pasture (comfort zone). Understand that you must leave them there if you desire to pursue your dreams.

212 Don't be so tunnel-visioned on rebuking people in their circumstances that you're too blind to see God revealed it to you to restore the people and bring them out of their circumstances.

213 You'll never be 100% ready for what's coming; just be 100% committed. Perfect circumstances are not necessary, but what is necessary is perfect commitment.

214 You can't wait until an opportunity comes to prepare. You have to already be prepared when the opportunity comes.

215 If you never live in your true identity, you'll never make the indentation (mark, impression) God created you to make.

216 Remember, relationships must have reciprocity. Otherwise, you don't have a relationship, you have an arrangement.

217 Have you put yourself in a position to be positioned? Have you done your part?

218 Spiritual Warfare only comes when you step out of comfort and into destiny and purpose.

219 How long will you pray and pray and pray and not pursue? It's pray without ceasing, not pray so I can cease doing!

220 Don't expect change, progress, or success in the areas in which you are unwilling to sacrifice. Instead prepare for stagnation, status quo, and mediocrity.

221 A vision unspoken will remain an unsupported idea until it is shared. No one knows there is the seed of a rose in the ground until it decides to break out of the earth and bloom, showing its beauty and splendor to the world.

222 Sometimes the best way to wake people up is to shake them. Oftentimes challenge is the only means by which change can occur. Don't be afraid to shake things up.

223 Vision is more about the future so don't get discouraged by the past. It's about the manifestation of the thoughts God had concerning you even when you were still a concept in his imagination. It's about becoming the true you.

224 Be careful of allying yourself with someone who permits you to quit easily. You'll subconsciously learn to run from challenges instead of confronting them and conquering them.

225 When you isolate yourself, you shut out any voice of encouragement and subsequently allow the enemy's voice to be louder than anything else. Predators prey on those who are alone.

226 Your vision will be mere thoughts unless you take the necessary steps to make it a reality. If the steps are never taken, those mere thoughts will ultimately become sure regret.

227 Church is not only a place you go to; it is also an influence and government you bring to the world. Ecclesia (the called out and sent ones).

228 Satan is not threatened by people who are stationary. Only those that are moving into their call demand his attention. If you're in your comfort zone, then so is Satan.

229 When you're committed, it doesn't matter what happens along the way because you are willing to go through the process and take the hits you need to take to accomplish the mission.

230 There's a difference between quitting and failing. One is a matter of the mind and heart. The other is a matter of wisdom and strength. When you have the mind and you have the heart to keep going, the wisdom and strength you need are inevitable.

231 Deliver the message just as God packaged it; don't worry about re-wrapping it in bows and ribbons so that it is appealing to the addressee. You just might *conceal* what God wants to *reveal*.

232 Never argue over hypotheticals. Never give a self-constructed theory the power of reality. Never give fiction the power of facts. You'll save time, energy, and sanity.

233 Reject the relax, rest, and be raptured approach to Kingdom living. As a matter of fact that's not Kingdom living at all. This Gospel shall be preached in all the world.

234 Keep someone on your team that challenges you to a point that you almost hate them during the rehearsal, but you appreciate them when you face the real test because they've prepared you for it.

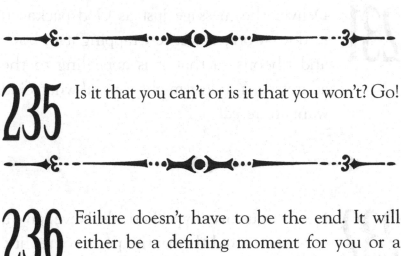

235 Is it that you can't or is it that you won't? Go!

236 Failure doesn't have to be the end. It will either be a defining moment for you or a stepping stone to an opportunity to get better. You choose!

237 The success of a leader is not measured by how well he dominates; it is measured by how well he motivates.

238 Repetition makes you a good actor, but revelation changes the heart and mindset.

239 Even when they are winning, champions always look for ways to improve and grow. That is the difference that sets champions apart from those that simply have talent. Champions never stop learning and never stop growing.

240 You can be good by being approximate (round about, somewhere in the area, almost), but to be excellent you must be precise (exact, targeted, aimed in, bull's-eye).

241 Being courageous doesn't mean you have an absence of fear. Actually, fear is an ingredient of courage. Courage means you have awareness of the uncertainty or danger and still take a risk and confront your fear.

242 Anyone who compromises what is right for the sake of keeping peace will never make a difference! It's only those who stand up for what is right who shift the culture of a generation and generations to come.

243 You are the canvas, He is the artist. Denying greatness in yourself is to deny the greatness in God because you were created in His image and likeness. You are the work of His hands.

244 Others are the beneficiaries of my dreams. It is a privilege to pull out the potential in others to push them into empowerment and purpose.

245 Missions are about going where you are needed not only where you are comfortable. Paul suffered stripes, shipwrecks, and imprisonment half his life to get to those who needed him most. Go to those who need what you carry inside of you.

246 If you never push the limits, then you shouldn't expect to experience progress. The boundaries you set within your own mind will hold you hostage if you don't push the limits with new goals that cause you to reach higher. You CAN!

247 God is Alpha and Omega, who *was* (past) and *is* (present) and *is to come* (future). When you realize that God Is eternal and limitless and that you are his child, you'll never worry about lack again.

248 The mark of those who are committed to you isn't those who are around most frequently. The marks of commitment are those that are still by your side and faithful in the face of adversity. When the storm comes and the dust settles, look up to see who is still with you.

249 Don't mistake unity to mean sameness. God designed you to be different. It is your differences in harmony with one another that create the perfect team of individuals.

250 Just as a rubber band must be stretched in order to spring forward to the direction in which you point it; likewise, we must be stretched to be launched into divine destiny. Don't quit while God is stretching you; he is about to launch you.

251 Grace is getting what you do not deserve, like forgiveness and eternal life.

Mercy is *not* getting what you *do* deserve, like condemnation and eternal damnation.

252 Some of us are wondering why God hasn't filled us lately. Could it possibly be because you have not poured out what He has given you to begin with? God gives bread to the eater and seed to the sower. You are like God's distribution center, but your inventory may be overstocked. Pour out!

253 If all your friends and associates look like, act like, talk like, and come from the same places as you; then you likely don't live a life of much influence. Your life perspectives and life experiences are likely shallow, at best.

254 God himself went out of his way, put himself in your place, and died on your behalf so that he could rescue you and have a relationship with you. If he did all of that just for you, then why do you think so lowly of yourself?

255 When the devil wants to *stop* you, he brings up your past to try to discourage you and postpone the future God has predestined for you. When God wants to *use* you, he uses your past as a pedestal to stand on to *promote* you into your purpose.

256 Sometimes it does not matter what people's opinions are or what they say. Sometimes God has said all the saying that needs to be said. If you look in all directions for guidance, then you are bound to get lost. But there is assurance in looking to God.

257 Forgiveness is just as much for the person doing the forgiving as it is for the forgiven. Drop the weight of the baggage of resentment and pick up freedom and joy. Free yourself and forgive them. Unforgiveness of the past things is a robber of the enjoyment of the present things.

258 Sometimes in Christianity we focus too much on what we can't do anymore now that we're Christians and too little on what we can now do just because we're Christians. Willpower versus the power of the Holy Spirit. Go from following rules and regulations to just simply ruling and regulating by God's power.

259 Surround yourself with geniuses. It's okay to connect with someone that's strong where you are weak. You don't have to feel threatened by people who can contribute at the same level or higher than yourself. If one succeeds, then you both do. If you're always the smartest, most talented person in the group, then you set yourself up for stagnation and complacency.

260 You should be aware of what's going on around you. The moment you only know what's going on in your circle of people then how can God influence the world through you? Make a conscious effort to be relevant enough to reach others. That is not compromise, that is wisdom and strategy. He who wins souls is wise. Proverbs 11:30

261 Everyone has 24 hours in a day. You have to be intentional on how you *spend* your time. Time is a currency, once you spend it you don't get it back unless you have invested wisely. People that are going somewhere always value time.

262 A fish doesn't struggle at swimming. A bird doesn't struggle at flying. A hound doesn't struggle at hunting. They just do what they do because it's what they were created to do; it's in their DNA. You are sons of God, stop struggling to be what you already are. Just *be*!

263 You can't do the minimum and reach your maximum potential. That math doesn't add up. Success is seized outside of normalcy.

264 It's easy to find the excuse readily available to you. It's more challenging to dig deep and discover the excellence hidden within you.

265 At some point before successful people become successful, someone thought they were crazy—until they succeeded.

266 The solution is always greater than the problem.

267 Motivation gets you going, commitment keeps you from stopping.

268 Never allow yourself to be a victim in your way of thinking. We are more than conquerors, according to Romans 8:37.

269 God has created you to be an answer to the most desperate prayers. You are an extension of the kingdom of heaven. Acts 9:10-12

270 It's dangerous to place value in everybody's opinion. Only permit a few trusted people with that much power to validate the direction your life is headed.

PART II
SELAH
THOUGHTS, REFLECTIONS, AND MEDITATIONS

Jeremiah 29:11 New King James Version
For I know the thoughts that I think toward
you, says the Lord, thoughts of peace and not
of evil, to give you a future and a hope.

271 God does not give small visions. He gives impossible visions that are only possible by His divine favor, grace, strength, and wisdom. It's almost like He shows you, then dares you to believe it can be accomplished through Him.

Anything that can be accomplished short of miraculous intervention may be a hobby, but I doubt it's the full vision.

272 The higher you build the more important your foundation becomes.

You can only build as high as the foundation is able to support. If you desire to build something great, then make sure you have a great support system.

273 In mathematics you can do steps correctly, but if it's not in the right *order* you'll still get the wrong answer. You have to follow the formula. When you follow the formula step-by-step, you always get the right answer.

Likewise, you can be doing all the right things. However, if it's not in God's order or timing, you can find yourself outside of his will.

274 You must take a risk to be successful. However, risk without a plan or strategy to carry it out is not a risk at all; that's called gambling.

Risk: Possibilities based on well-calculated chance and strategy. Possibilities and preparation make it probable.

Gamble: Based on nothing more that unlikely luck. It's possible but not probable.

275 The first step to change or reaching goals is a determined mindset.

Mindset: *Mind* + *Set* = to have the mind *set* or fixed. Literally to have the mind fixed, dialed in to a predetermined outcome. Having your mind set and decided on a specific goal or outcome and not stopping until you reach the benchmark.

276 God's plan was never to get you to go to Heaven. God's plan was to bring Heaven to Earth and make his home amongst us. God did not create man and place him in Heaven with him. Instead he made man, placed him on Earth and came to him (Genesis 2, 3). In Revelation 21, God brings New Jerusalem to Earth thus making heaven on Earth.

From the beginning of time God yearned to be with you—from Eden to New Jerusalem.

277 One of the most valuable things in life is time. Many things can be replaced or refunded, but your time is not one of them. Many times where we are in life or where we are not in life are direct results of what we've done with our time. There is only one of two things you can do with time—invest it or waste it. People who value purpose *always* value their time.

278 Faith and obedience are synonymous in the word of God.

You have to have faith to obey and you have to be obedient to show your faith.

If you don't obey God, it is evident that you do not have faith in what He has said.

You will act on what you believe, and you won't act in what you do not trust.

Hypothetically speaking, If God has given you a vision and has told you to do A, B, and C to make it come to pass, and you do not obey it; it is evident that there is no faith at work. On the other hand, if you do obey what He has said, then your faith is made known.

Remember when faith is at work, obedience must also be present. It's like heads and tails on a coin they go together.

Faith without works is dead!

279 When you think big, you can't associate with small minds.

The reality is some don't have the capacity to think extraordinarily because their minds are calibrated to comprehend normalcy. Big thinkers imagine their possibilities, but small minds can't think past their limitations.

280 An alarm clock is designed to alert you to begin your day. When we keep pushing snooze, we subsequently delay the start of our day and shorten the window of opportunity of the day.

Likewise, some of us keep sleeping on our goals and pushing them back when we know it's time to *go*.

Procrastination. Prohibits. Progress.

281 If God answered your prayers today would you be prepared to receive it or would it overwhelm and destroy you? If we are honest, sometimes we pray for things we are not prepared to manage. It's too big to handle in our current condition, at times. We pray for big ideas but don't want to take on the big endeavors it takes to handle big things. Maybe, just maybe, it's by God's grace that some of our prayers don't get answered. Don't just talk about it. Get ready for it.

282 There are only two ways that you respond when you are convicted by the truth.

The first is humbly, with an *openness* to change.

The second is prideful, closed off and with *opposition* to change.

283 In the past an altar was a place where one thing died so that another could live. It was ugly, there was bloodshed. It was where you brought your sacrifice in an attempt to satisfy what you owed but could not fully pay yourself. However, when you come to the new covenant altar (the Cross of Christ), there will be no more dying because Jesus has done the dying once and for all! There will be no bloodshed because Jesus shed his blood on your behalf so you don't have to. There will be no more sacrifice acquired and offered by the works your own hands because he was the ultimate sacrifice! There will be no debt to fulfill because he paid the price!

284 In the rules of mathematics I learned that a negative multiplied by another negative equals a positive. I never understood why, but I am convinced that life, at times, works the same way.

Romans 8:28 proclaims, "And we know that all things work together for good to those who love God, to those who are the called according to his purpose."

285 God split the Red Sea to bring Israel *out of* Egypt, and he did the very same thing to the Jordan River to bring Israel *into* the Promised Land!

It was God's hand that brought you out of your past life (Egypt). The same God will take you into your future (Promised Land).

286 If you want to enlarge your territory, you must be willing to go into territory that's foreign to what you're used to. You must expose yourself to different cultures, different perspectives, different atmospheres, different paradigms, different terminology, different environments, different people, and different social statuses.

Sometimes you have to fight the urge to draw close to those who are like you. Instead, intentionally engage with something or someone that forces you to grow.

287 Everyone visualizes what the end result of their goal would look like. The problem is many of us get frustrated and quit before we get there. Let me encourage and remind you to celebrate the small victories on your journey until you reach your goal or finished product. An artist chips away little by little, bit by bit until he chisels the masterpiece that he visualized from the beginning!

288 There are 3 types of people you cannot help even if you tried:

1. The hard-hearted: people who simply don't want to change or who do not welcome your help or advice
2. The unteachable: people who think they are smarter than you and think they can do everything better than you

3. The uncommitted: people who want change but are unwilling to do what it takes to achieve change

289 TURBULENCE

Have you noticed that when you travel by plane taking off is the most turbulent part? Even though you feel the turbulence, you have to keep in mind that you are going somewhere and have a destination to reach! What you'll also notice is that ultimately, the turbulence subsides as you go higher and higher in elevation.

The moral of the story? There is turbulence when you take off, start, or transition to higher dimensions and higher levels. Don't let the turbulence stop you in between transition into higher levels. Don't worry, everything will smooth out eventually. Keep going!

290 THE DIFFERENCE

Water is very hot at 211 degrees, but at 212 degrees it reaches a boiling point. Think about that *one degree* difference and it reaches its *full potential*. One degree difference produces enough power to set a steam engine train into motion. What is your one degree? What is that one thing you need to turn up in your life to maximize and manifest the *more* in you?

291 ABOVE

Once I was on a flight. The plane began to shake violently by turbulence due to a storm. The pilot came over the PA system and said, "Ladies and gentleman, we are experiencing some turbulence because we are going through a storm." He then said, "Relax, we are going to climb to a higher altitude and fly over the storm."

Oftentimes, I hear people confess that they are going through storm after storm. Well sometimes it is not God's will that you keep going through storms. He created you to climb higher and fly over the storm! We are more than conquerors!

292 CLIMATE

According to www.dictionary.com, climate is defined as prevailing weather conditions of a region, as temperature, air pressure, humidity, precipitation, sunshine, cloudiness, and winds, throughout the year, averaged over a series of years.

—Synonyms
Mood, ATMOSPHERE, spirit, TONE, temper.

I would like to address your spiritual climate. One thing I want you to notice about climate is that it provides the right atmosphere for certain vegetation to grow. Certain plants and animals need certain types of climates to survive and flourish. The climate creates the atmosphere that provides the ingredients necessary for that particular species. Another thing to notice is if a certain animal or plant is in the wrong climate, it will have no chance at life at all. If you place a palm tree in a frigid climate, it will surely die. Likewise, if you put an animal that is meant to live in a tropical climate in the desert or arctic atmosphere it will die.

The reason it dies is because it is in an atmosphere that does not provide the necessary nutrients or conditions it needs to stay alive, and without those necessities it will die.

One thing that influences a region's climate is its positioning on earth. For example, the climate in Florida is different than that of Texas. The climate of Arizona is different than that of Alaska. In other words, people have to be in the right position with God to have a healthy spiritual climate.

Mankind was created to be in the presence of God (Eden). The climate in Eden (his presence) will provide an atmosphere for you to flourish. That's why the Bible says things like, "In his presence there is fullness of joy," "In his presence there is peace." The climate of God will provide the right atmosphere for you to flourish and go higher in him. But the climate of the world will cause your spirit to die. Ladies and gentlemen, climate causes things to come into order. If you want revival, then the climate has to be right for revival. If you want growth, then the climate has to be right for growth.

293 PAINTBRUSH

The most valuable property a paintbrush has is not the quality of wood, nor is it the texture of the bristles. The most valuable characteristic in the eyes of the artist is that the brush completely yields itself in his hands. The brush does not resist, it just allows the artist to guide it with his hand. The end result is something that we call a masterpiece. In other words, if we would just yield our lives to the master and let his hand guide us like the paintbrush allows the artist to guide it, then we will be in his perfect will. Thus producing his work of art and creating his masterpiece.

Learn a lesson from the paintbrush. Submit to God and be led by his Spirit.

John 16:13 says, "Howbeit when he, the Spirit of truth, is come, he will guide you into all truth: for he shall not speak of himself; but whatsoever he shall hear, that shall he speak: and he will shew you things to come."

294 THE SEED

In order for a seed to grow, it first has to be buried in fertile soil.

The question that I have for you is, "Have you died to yourself so that you may be buried in Christ?" According to www.dictionary. com being buried is defined as "to plunge in deeply, cause to sink in, cover in order to conceal from sight, to immerse." Christ is the fertile soil, you are the seed. Have you ever seen a seed growing without being buried in soil? In most cases, no! The interesting thing about a seed is that it is so small, yet it has all the potential within itself to become a great plant or a tree. The soil is what brings the potential out of the seed. The seed is nothing but a shell to what is within it. In other words Christ will cause you to come out of your shell. What's also interesting is within the definition of the word buried, it also mentions being buried means "*to cover as to conceal from sight*". If you have not been buried in Christ, the world will continue to see you and not Christ the King.

2 Corinthians 5:17 states, Therefore if any man be IN Christ, he is a new creature: old things are passed away; behold, all things are become new."

295 ADHESIVE

Adhesive means of or pertaining to the molecular force that exists in the area of contact between unlike bodies that acts to unite them.

When I think of the definition of this word adhesive it makes me think of what the blood of Christ does for us. The blood of Christ being the molecular force. The definition indicates that an adhesive is the binding agent between unlike bodies. God is so holy, so righteous, so worthy. Naturally, we are separated from him because we are sinful, thus in that aspect we are unlike. But I love the way the definition says that an adhesive acts to unite the two separate objects. The blood of Christ is the adhesive that binds us to a father and a friend that we were separated from because of sin. The blood of Christ is the adhesive to bind us back into union with Him. We were originally created in God's image and likeness; thank God for the adhesive power of the blood! You have been glued to the King of Kings!

Ephesians 2:13-14
But now in Christ Jesus you who once were far away have been brought near through the blood of Christ. For he himself is our peace, who has made the two one and has destroyed the barrier, the dividing wall of hostility,

296

ANARCHY

According to www.dictionary.com anarchy means chaos, disorder, confusion, the absence of government and law

When I looked up this word it dawned on me that the kingdom of God is a government. If anarchy is the absence of government, order or law this would indicate that those areas in our lives that we have not submitted to the kingdom of God are subject to anarchy. Those areas that are out of order, chaotic, and confusing are the results of not having the government of God in that area.

I remember when I first gave my life to Christ, and God started to shape my life. I also remember that the areas that I had the most confusion and chaos in were the areas that were not fully surrendered to God. In other words I tried to hold on to some of my will and desires, and it created anarchy in that area of my life. Let the Holy Spirit be the governor of your life in every area.

297

NEIGHBOR

I saw a commercial from State farm Insurance, and the catch phrase was this, "Like a good neighbor, State Farm is there"

Today I would like to rewrite the song. "Like a good neighbor THE CHURCH is there."

I would like to pose a question to all ministers of the Gospel.

The question is this: Is your ministry a neighbor to the community in which you are planted? Or does the community only know your ministry as the church on the corner?

If you don't know the answer to that question, I'll ask you a few more questions that may help reveal the facts to you.

Would the community in which you are planted even notice if you were to close the doors to the church and move? Would the community be devastated by your absence or would they go on as they always have?

if the city tried to close your ministry, would the community in which you are planted petition the city or even try to intercede on the church's behalf?

If you were to close, would the community you serve say, "What happened to _____ church?"

Lastly, if your ministry were taken out of the community in which you are planted, would there be an obvious void in that community without the function of your ministry or church?

If you answered no to those questions, then your ministry is not making a difference in the community that God placed you in. You have just become another church on the corner!

Let us become good neighbors!

298 STORM STORY (TESTIMONY)

For those of you that know me personally, you know that I travel often.

I was on a long road trip listening to music and talking on the phone. It was a sunny day; but as I was driving, in the distance I could see a huge, dark, violent looking cloud. I said to myself, "Man, I'm headed into a storm." This is when God started to give me revelation on trials (AKA storms). Sometimes when we are approaching a storm, God will allow us to see it at a distance. In some cases He may be warning you to turn around; in some cases he may be telling you to get prepared.

As I got closer to this storm the sky got darker and darker and darker, then *boom*, I was going through the storm. Notice I said *going* through the storm not *sitting* in the storm. As I was going through the storm, you could barely see as the water and hail pounded my windshield, but I kept going. Although, my ability to see where I was going was temporarily obscured. I also noticed that some cars stopped and sat idle on the side of the road. That's when I noticed when you sit still in a storm, you increase your time in the storm.

Remember I told you that before I went into the storm I was listening to music and talking on the phone? Well, as I was in the storm I ejected my music and put my phone down. I tuned into the radio and began listening to the weather channel to hear what was going on and what I needed to do. I realized that at that moment the music and the phone were worthless to me; the voice that I really needed to hear was the broadcaster. The broadcaster will tell you where the danger is coming from and tell you what you need to do (take cover, keep going, etc.). I said all that to let you know that God will allow a storm to come upon you so that you may tune in to him and get rid of the distractions. In times of spiritual storm we need to hear the voice of the broadcaster, who is God. He will tell you what you need to do, where danger is coming from, and will lead you through the storm.

As I kept going through the storm, the sky in the horizon became brighter and brighter and brighter. It also began to rain less and less. That's when I noticed that God was showing me that the Son (Jesus) would still be with me during spiritual storms. Then suddenly, I saw the actual sun when I came out on the other side of the storm. There was peace where the sun was. Looking in my rearview mirror, I saw that massive storm behind me, and I saw some cars still sitting idle in the storm. The difference between me and the cars sitting in the storm is that they were not listening to the broadcaster. They did not know what to do in the storm! But I did listen to the broadcaster. He said, "I know things are chaotic, but there are no tornadoes coming so keep going.' Listen to God in the time of storm; he will tell you what to do! If not, you will keep going when he says take cover, or you will be taking cover and idling when he says keep going!

Remember that the Son is with you in the storm! Tune in to him.

299

CORRECTION

I've often heard people say, "I wasn't getting fed at that church." And if you've ever said it yourself, I'd like to share a quick thought with you. In the New Testament there was a time when there were 12 disciples who eventually graduated to the Apostles. In other words, they went from students to teachers. They went from consumers to contributors. They went from being fed to being responsible for feeding others. What I'm saying is the reason your spirit may feel unfulfilled or unsatisfied is because you may still be in the pews seeking to consume when God is pushing you to start contributing. It's not always all about you *getting* something. Sometimes it's about you *giving* something. Could you imagine what things would be like if the Apostles waited around for someone to feed them after Jesus ascended?

The truth is that at one time, the disciples' only responsibility was to be fed. However, there eventually came a day when they were responsible for providing meals! They had become the feeder and not solely the eater.

300 I am the clay but he is the potter.
I am the instrument but He is the orchestrator.
I am the paint but He is the brush.
I am the canvas but he is the artist.
I am the chisel but He is the hammer.
I am the microphone but he is the voice.
We are the body but he is the mind!

Printed in the United States
By Bookmasters